# BASEBALL

MADISON PARKER

Rourke
Educational Media

rourkeeducationalmedia.com

# TABLE OF CONTENTS

Get Psyched!......................................................4

Game On............................................................6

Suit Up! .........................................................12

Through the Years ..........................................16

Science in Baseball........................................20

Where in the World? .......................................24

Play Ball!........................................................28

Glossary .........................................................30

Index................................................................31

Show What You Know .....................................31

Websites to Visit ............................................31

About the Author ...........................................32

# GET PSYCHED!

You swing the bat. Crack! The ball soars into the **outfield**.

You run to first **base**. Then second, then third, then to home plate. It's a home run! You are psyched to play baseball!

## HOME RUN HOOPLA

Some Major League Baseball (MLB) stadiums have unique ways to celebrate home runs. The New York Mets have an apple that pops out of a top hat. The San Francisco Giants shoot off fireworks while they play the sound of a foghorn. The Houston Astros have a train loaded with oranges that travels slowly across the wall from center to left field.

# GAME ON

Baseball is a team sport played by people of all ages. It is popular in the United States and around the world.

## GAME ON!

To entertain crowds between innings, many stadiums have people in costumes race around the field. The Milwaukee Brewers have a sausage race. Presidents run around the bases at Washington Nationals games.

Play ball! To score points, the batter hits the ball and runs around the bases to home plate. The **fielders** try to catch the ball and stop the batter and other runners from getting back to home plate.

A baseball game lasts nine innings. The defense starts on the field. The offense is "at bat."

Offense

Defense

Do the Math:
if both teams are at bat in each inning, what is the total number of at bats in a regular nine inning game?
(Answer: 2 x 9 = 18)

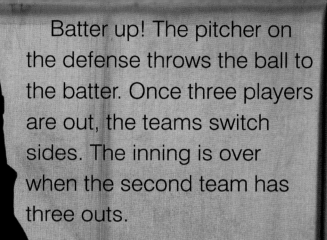

Batter up! The pitcher on the defense throws the ball to the batter. Once three players are out, the teams switch sides. The inning is over when the second team has three outs.

## GAME ON!

There are a few ways to make an out. A batter can strike out by swinging the bat but not hitting the ball three times. Fielders can catch balls that are hit into the air, or a player on base can catch a ball before the runner gets to that base.

A baseball field has two areas. The **infield** has lines that connect the bases to home plate. The pitcher is in a circle called the pitcher's mound.

OUTFIELD GRASS

INFIELD

FOUL LINE

PITCHER'S MOUND

FOUL LINE

HOME PLATE

Going, going, gone to the outfield! The outfield is the part of the field that has grass. It is outside of the infield.

## GAME ON!

The umpire is the ruler of the diamond. He or she stands behind home plate and decides whether pitches are strikes or balls. The umpire also decides if a runner is safe or out at a base.

# SUIT UP!

Wearing the right clothes helps you play better. Most baseball jerseys have short sleeves to be comfortable.

## GAME ON!

Clothing designers create unique uniforms for special games. Each year on April 15, all MLB players wear the number 42 to honor Jackie Robinson, the first African American to play professional baseball.

(1919–1972)

When sliding into a base, it is good that baseball pants are tight! Long socks are worn under the pants. Players also wear helmets when batting and running the bases. On their feet, players wear cleats, which help dig into the field for more grip.

Safe! Batters need bats and helmets to play. Fielders need small gloves to catch the ball. Pitchers need a baseball to throw to the batter.

## HEAD GEAR

A batting helmet is a hard plastic hat worn over a player's baseball cap. It protects the player from getting injured by fast-moving baseballs.

Catchers have to catch balls flying faster than cars driving on the highway! They wear large gloves with extra padding. They also wear a helmet, face mask, chest protector, and shin guards.

## GAME ON!

Many baseballs are made with cork in the middle. Yarn or twine is then wrapped around the cork. White leather goes around the ball and is attached with red stitches.

How old is baseball? More than 200 years ago, the British colonists brought games played with a bat and ball to the colonies. These games were called cricket and rounders.

Cricket is a game played with a bat and ball between two teams. One team bats and tries to score runs. The other team bowls and fields the ball.

*Alexander Cartwright in later life as a fire chief. (1820–1892)*

Alexander Cartwright made a **variation** of those games and called it baseball. On June 19, 1846, the first official baseball game in the United States was played using these new rules.

## THE TRUTH

Some people think Abner Doubleday (1819–1893) invented baseball in a cow field in Cooperstown, New York, in 1839. However, this story is untrue. Doubleday was still studying at the U.S. Military Academy at West Point in 1839. Even Doubleday himself never claimed to have anything to do with the game!

*Antique baseball glove from the 1800s.*

The National League was formed with eight teams in 1876. The American League was formed with eight teams in 1901.

*National League Baltimore Orioles, 1896*

Do the Math:
How many years later was the American League formed than the National League?
(Answer: 1901 – 1876 = 25)

## THIS GIRL'S GOT GAME!

In 2015, Melissa Mayeux, a shortstop on the French U-18 junior national team, became the first female baseball player to be added to the MLB's international registration list. This makes her eligible to be signed by a major league club.

Both leagues now have three divisions. Each division has five teams. With 30 teams in the MLB in the U.S. and Canada, there is likely one close by!

*The Boston Red Soxs and Toronto Blue Jays are both in the American League.*

# SCIENCE IN BASEBALL

Your body has super powers! Pitchers use **physics** to throw a fast ball. They get more **energy** into the ball by rotating their hips and then their shoulders as they throw the ball.

*A pitcher can spin the ball to add topspin, backspin, or sidespin. After leaving a pitcher's hand, the pitch is influenced by gravity and drag.*

A batter's eyes, brain, and muscles must work together to swing the bat to hit the ball. Energy moves from the muscles to the bat and then to the ball.

## GAME ON!

After breaking his bat, major league Louisville Eclipse player Pete Browning was invited by 17-year-old Bud Hillerich to come to his father's woodworking shop. Bud handcrafted a new bat with Browning giving him advice. The next day, Browning got three hits. His teammates went to the shop to get their own specially made bats. In 1894, the name "Louisville Slugger" was registered with the U.S. Patent office.

Watch this! Pitchers and batters record their practices. They **analyze** their moves by watching their performances to improve their level of play.

# TRAMPOLINE EFFECT

The walls of an aluminum bat are thin. They flex when the ball hits the bat. Some of the energy of the collision is transferred into the bat instead of the ball. That energy bounces back and gives more energy to the ball.

Some players like to use aluminum bats because of the trampoline effect. The ball is hit faster and farther.

# WHERE IN THE WORLD?

Canadians enjoy playing baseball during the warmth of the summer. The Toronto Blue Jays are an MLB team.

## IT'S OUTTA HERE!

Babe Ruth's first home run was hit into the water outside Hanlan's Point Stadium in Toronto, Ontario. Some people think the ball is still in the water.

(1895–1948)

# DOMINICAN CHAMPS

The Dominican Republic has produced four MVP winners: Sammy Sosa, Miguel Tejada, Vladimir Guerrero, and Albert Pujols.

Sammy Sosa

Miguel Tejada

Vladimir Guerrero

Albert Pujols

The Dominican Republic has the most players active in the MLB and the two largest summer leagues outside of the U.S.

The first professional league in Japan was created in 1936. It is called Nippon Professional Baseball (NPB). There are many Japanese nationals who play for MLB teams.

*The Hiroshima Toyo Carp take on the Yokohama Baystars. Both teams are part of the NPB.*

When the U.S. Army Air Corps was stationed in Manipur, India, during World War II, the troops introduced the locals to baseball. To promote the game, the Amateur Baseball Federation of India was created in 1983. On July 4, 2009, Rinku Singh became the first Indian citizen to play in an MLB game. He was discovered on a reality show called *Million Dollar Arm*.

*Rinku Singh*

## GAME ON!

Sports agent J.B. Bernstein thought a cricket bowler could become a baseball pitcher. Cricket is a game similar to baseball that is popular in India. He created *Million Dollar Arm*. The reality show winner would get the opportunity to be on an MLB team and win $100,000.

# PLAY BALL!

Baseball players have to do many things to be successful. They practice regularly and listen to their coaches. They keep their bodies strong by eating healthy foods and working out.

## Coach's notes:
- Arrive to practice on time
- Eat a healthy meal before practice
- Get enough sleep
- Do your best on and off the field
- Respect everyone

## GIVING BACK

Many professional players give back to their communities. Former Yankee All Star Derek Jeter created the Turn 2 Foundation to promote positive lifestyles for kids. He also hosts fundraisers including a celebrity golf tournament in Tampa, Florida. Jeter often returns to his hometown of Kalamazoo, Michigan, to support local kids with scholarships and baseball clinics.

Are you psyched to play baseball?

## GAME ON!

"Take Me Out to the Ball Game" is sung during the middle of the seventh inning of a baseball game. The lyrics were written by Jack Norworth in 1908 while he was riding a subway train. Composer Albert Von Tizer wrote the music. Jack saw his first baseball game 32 years later. Albert saw his first baseball game 20 years later.

# GLOSSARY

**analyze** (AH-nuh-lize): to study something in a careful way

**base** (BAYS): one of the four places a runner has to touch to get a point

**energy** (EH-nuhr-jee): force or power

**fielders** (FEEL-duhrs): players who try to catch a ball

**infield** (IN-feeld): the area on the baseball field that includes the four bases and the pitcher's mound

**outfield** (OUT-feeld): the area on the baseball field behind first, second, and third bases

**physics** (FIH-zihks): the scientific study of matter and energy

**variation** (vayr-ee-AY-shun): a slightly different version of something

# INDEX

American League  18, 19

batter(s )  7, 9, 14, 21, 22

Cartwright,  Alexander 17

catchers  15

defense  8, 9

Dominican  Republic 25

field  5, 6, 8, 10, 11

fielders  7, 9, 14

Jeter, Derek  28

Mayeux, Melissa  18

National League  18

physics  20

pitcher(s)  9, 10, 14, 20, 22

trampoline effect  23

# SHOW WHAT YOU KNOW

1. Which side bats first in an inning?
2. Who developed the modern game of baseball?
3. How is physics important in baseball?
4. What countries have professional baseball leagues?
5. How many innings are played in a game?

# WEBSITES TO VISIT

www.sciencebuddies.org

www.mlb.com

www.baseballyouth.com

# ABOUT THE AUTHOR

Madison Parker lives with her husband and three sons in New York. When she isn't writing books, you will find her outside playing all kinds of sports with her family. Her favorite baseball teams are the New York Yankees and the Hudson Valley Renegades.

**Meet The Author!**
www.meetREMauthors.com

www.rourkeeducationalmedia.com

PHOTO CREDITS: Cover, title page: Pali Rao; page 3: ©Greg Hadel; page 5: ©fredrocko; page 5 (bottom): ©Cpenter; page 6: ©Colleen Butler; page 6 (bottom): ©Wisconsinart; page 7: ©Andrea Pelletier; page 7 (bottom): ©Michael Ciu; page 8: ©Michael Ciu; page 9, 13: ©Donald Miralle; page 10: ©Walleyelj; page 11: ©quavondo; page 12: ©PPGGutenbergUKLtd; page 14: ©Mike Watson; page 15: ©Joseph Gareri; page 17: ©Rijerion; page 17 (top): ©Hawaii State Archives; page 18: ©JGHowes; page 19: Dennis Ku; page 20: ©Michael Svoboda; page 21: ©Judy LynnBarranco; page 21 (bottom): ©Wikipedia; page 22: ©Willowpix; page 23: RBFried; page 25: ©Charles Sollars Concepts; page 26: ©Sean Pavone; page 27: ©HelgaEsteb; page 28: ©Vadym Drobot; page 28 (bottom): ©Jamie McCarthy

Edited by: Keli Sipperley
Cover design by: Rhea Magaro
Interior design by: Jen Thomas

### Library of Congress PCN Data

Baseball / Madison Parker
(Game On! Psyched For Sports)
ISBN (hard cover)(alk. paper) 978-1-68191-755-9
ISBN (soft cover) 978-1-68191-856-3
ISBN (e-Book) 978-1-68191-946-1
Library of Congress Control Number: 2016932717

Printed in the United States of America,
Conover, North Carolina